Clifton Park - Halfmoon Public Library
475 Moe Road
Clifton Park, New York 12065

The History of INDEPENDENCE DAY

By Reese Donaghey

Gareth Stevens
PUBLISHING

Please visit our website, www.garethstevens.com. For a free color catalog of all our high-quality books, call toll free 1-800-542-2595 or fax 1-877-542-2596.

Library of Congress Cataloging-in-Publication Data

Donaghey, Reese.
The history of Independence Day / by Reese Donaghey.
p. cm. — (What you didn't know about history)
Includes index.
ISBN 978-1-4824-1942-9 (pbk.)
ISBN 978-1-4824-1941-2 (6-pack)
ISBN 978-1-4824-1943-6 (library binding)
1.Fourth of July — Juvenile literature. 2. Fourth of July celebrations — Juvenile literature. I. Donaghey, Reese. II. Title.
E286.D65 2015
394.2634—d23
6023

First Edition

Published in 2015 by
Gareth Stevens Publishing
111 East 14th Street, Suite 349
New York, NY 10003

Copyright © 2015 Gareth Stevens Publishing

Designer: Andrea Davison-Bartolotta
Editor: Kristen Rajczak

Photo credits: Cover, pp. 1, 19 (main) LOC.gov; p. 4 Mediagram/Shutterstock.com; p. 5 spirit of america/Shutterstock.com; p. 7 SuperStock/Getty Images; p. 9 (inset) VisionsofAmerica/ Joe Sohm/Photodisc/Getty Images; p. 9 (main) Stock Montage/Archive Photos/Getty Images; p. 10 David Smart/Shutterstock.com; p. 11 (inset) Andrew Burton/Getty Images; p. 11 (main) Universal Images Group/Getty Images; pp. 13, 19 (inset) Popperfoto/Getty Images; p. 15 DEA/M. Seemuller/DeAgostini/Getty Images; p. 17 Universal History Archive/ UIG/Getty Images; p. 20 lilyling1982/Shutterstock.com; p. 21 Gary C. Tognoni/ Shutterstock.com.

All rights reserved. No part of this book may be reproduced in any form without permission in writing from the publisher, except by a reviewer.

Printed in the United States of America

CPSIA compliance information: Batch #CW15GS: For further information contact Gareth Stevens, New York, New York at 1-800-542-2595.

CONTENTS

Words in the glossary appear in **bold** type the first time they are used in the text.

LET'S CELEBRATE!

For more than 230 years, the United States has been an independent nation. Every summer, there are parties on the Fourth of July, or Independence Day, to celebrate our freedom.

Most people know this date has something to do with the Declaration of Independence, which is the **document** declaring US freedom from Great Britain. But is July 4 the best date to **commemorate** it? In fact, there are many other dates on which Independence Day could be celebrated!

Did You Know?

"Declare" means "to announce." The Declaration of Independence was an announcement of freedom. To the British, it was an act of **rebellion!**

There are parades, picnics, and other events around the country to celebrate the Fourth of July.

ADAMS'S FIRST INDEPENDENCE DAY

By 1775, many of those living in the 13 British colonies in North America were unhappy. They felt like King George III of England wasn't giving them a voice in British government. So, **representatives** from each colony gathered in Philadelphia, Pennsylvania, in May 1775 to talk about what to do.

On May 12, they passed a **resolution** calling for all the colonies to write new **constitutions**. John Adams sometimes said May 15 was the *real* Independence Day because the resolution was finished that day.

Did You Know?
On May 15, John Adams added wording to the resolution in favor of trying for colonial independence.

The group that met in Philadelphia was called the Second Continental Congress. The first time the Continental Congress met was in 1774. They were trying to settle their problems with the British king then, too.

WRITING TIMELINE

You've likely learned that Thomas Jefferson was the main writer of the Declaration of Independence. He was, partly because he was known as a great writer. It was also because Benjamin Franklin and John Adams didn't want to do it!

These three men, in addition to Roger Sherman and Robert R. Livingston, made up the committee, or group, chosen to work on the document. Jefferson finished his first **draft** by the third week of June 1776. The others made changes over the next few weeks.

Did You Know?

In total, there were 86 changes made to Jefferson's original Declaration of Independence before it was finished.

You can still see an original printed copy of the Declaration of Independence! It's found at the National Museum of American History in Washington, DC.

Second of July

Independence Day could be celebrated on July 2, the day in 1776 when the Continental Congress voted to separate from England. In a letter, John Adams wrote, "The second day of July, 1776, will be the most memorable **epoch** in the history of America." While his idea was right, he was wrong about the date!

July 4, 1776, was the date the final draft of the Declaration of Independence was **approved**. It became known because the printer put that date clearly atop the printed document!

Did You Know?

Only 12 colonies voted for separation from England. New York abstained, or didn't vote.

Copies of the Declaration of Independence were handed out in the days following July 4. The Pennsylvania Evening Post *was the first newspaper to print it on July 6, 1776.*

Should August be called "Independence Month"? Though the representatives approved the final Declaration of Independence on July 4, none of them signed it until August 2—and some waited even longer to sign it.

The British might agree that August could be celebrated as the month of independence, too. Because mail had to cross an ocean by boat, the document didn't reach the king until the end of August 1776. The colonies would have considered themselves free almost 2 months before England even knew about it!

Did You Know?

Historians say all the representatives wouldn't have been present to sign the Declaration of Independence all at once. Most had jobs and families outside of Philadelphia to take care of.

This image is often said to show the signing of the Declaration of Independence. It's actually a painting of the committee presenting it to the Continental Congress for approval.

13

The first Independence Day celebration happened on July 8, 1776, in Philadelphia. The Declaration of Independence was read out loud for the first time, bells were rung around the city, and there was a parade. As word of colonial independence got around, other towns had celebrations, too. Some of them held **funerals** for King George!

The following year in Philadelphia, Independence Day was celebrated on July 4. Over the next few decades, similar celebrations became more common around the new country.

Did You Know?

The first Independence Day in Boston, Massachusetts, was on March 5, 1783. The city chose March 5 to commemorate the **Boston Massacre**, which occurred on that date in 1770.

After the Declaration of Independence was first read in New York City, colonists pulled down a statue of King George III!

HOLIDAY!

The Fourth of July was treated as a holiday long before it became one officially. In 1812, the United States went to war with Great Britain again. Copies of the Declaration of Independence were again given out to stir up **patriotism**. By the time the war ended, celebrating Independence Day had become popular.

It wasn't until 1870 that Congress established July 4 as a national holiday. It was part of a law that recognized many holidays, including Christmas and New Year's Day.

Did You Know?

In 1938, another law made July 4 a paid federal holiday. That means everyone who works for the government gets the day off and still gets paid! Many other businesses do this, too.

In 1876, the United States celebrated the centennial—or 100-year anniversary—of the Declaration of Independence with special July 4 parades and speeches.

17

WHAT'S IT CALLED?

When July 4 was declared a holiday, it wasn't given an official name. At first, the day was generally called Independence Day. By the end of the 1800s, "Fourth of July" became the most common name, and that's what the 1938 law listed the holiday as. This might seem silly now that you know that date is just one of many important dates on the nation's journey to independence.

Today, both names are used for the holiday that commemorates the colonies' declaration of freedom.

Did You Know?

During the 1800s, the Fourth of July was also called "Independent Day."

LET THE EAGLE SCREAM

HURRAH!   HURRAH!

4TH JULY

Fourth of July postcard from about 1900

Calvin Coolidge was president on the 150th anniversary celebration of the Declaration of Independence in 1926. It was also his 54th birthday!

LIGHT UP

Now common on the Fourth of July, the first fireworks were blown up on Independence Day 1777! They were lit on raised stages for all to see. The display began and ended with 13 fireworks, one for each of the 13 British colonies.

The spark for this celebration—and for ours today—is the freedom gained through the Declaration of Independence. Whether or not we commemorate it on the right day doesn't matter. That we're all able to show our patriotism and gratitude does!

Did You Know?
In 2013, about 175 million pounds (79 million kg) of fireworks were used in the United States to celebrate the Fourth of July.

Other Historical Events
of July 4

1817 — Work on the Erie Canal begins.

1826 — President John Adams and President Thomas Jefferson die.

1831 — President James Monroe dies.

1848 — The cornerstone of the Washington Monument is laid.

1872 — President Calvin Coolidge is born.

1946 — The Philippines is officially recognized as independent of the United States.

1960 — The modern flag with 50 stars is presented after the addition of Hawaii in 1959.

21

approve: to give official agreement

Boston Massacre: a fight between British troops and colonists in Boston, Massachusetts, on March 5, 1770

commemorate: to call to mind or mark an occasion

constitution: the basic laws by which a country or state is governed

document: a formal piece of writing

draft: the first try of a piece of writing

epoch: a period of time begun by a certain event

funeral: a ceremony to mark the burial of the dead

patriotism: love for one's country

rebellion: a fight to overthrow a government

representative: one who stands for a group of people

resolution: an official statement of purpose voted on by a group

FOR MORE INFORMATION

Books

Bowman, David. *What Would the Founding Fathers Say?* Springville, UT: Plain Sight Publishing, 2012.

Swain, Gwenyth. *Documents of Freedom: A Look at the Declaration of Independence, the Bill of Rights, and the U.S. Constitution.* Minneapolis, MN: Lerner Publications, 2012.

Websites

Fourth of July
www.socialstudiesforkids.com/subjects/4thofjuly.htm
Learn more about the Fourth of July and find links to games, crafts, and more on this website for kids.

History of the Fourth of July
www.history.com/topics/holidays/july-4th/videos/fourth-of-july-history
Watch a short video about the history of Independence Day.

Publisher's note to educators and parents: Our editors have carefully reviewed these websites to ensure that they are suitable for students. Many websites change frequently, however, and we cannot guarantee that a site's future contents will continue to meet our high standards of quality and educational value. Be advised that students should be closely supervised whenever they access the Internet.

Index